By Susan Holdaway
Illustrated by Edward Blake and Stephen Millingen

First published in 1994
by Anglia Young Books
Durhams Farmhouse
Ickleton
Saffron Walden, Essex CB10 1SR

© 1994 Susan Holdaway

All rights reserved. No part of this publication may be reproduced,
stored in a retrieval system, or transmitted in any form or by any means,
electronic, mechanical, photocopying, recording or otherwise
without the written permission of the publisher.

Illustrations by Edward Blake and Stephen Millingen

British Library Cataloguing-in-Publication Data

A catalogue record for this book is available from the British Library

ISBN 1 871173 30 2

Typeset in Futura and printed in Great Britain by
Redwood Books, Trowbridge, Wilts.

CONTENTS

	Page
FESTIVALS: An Introduction	5
CONFUCIANISM	6
THE FESTIVAL OF CHINESE NEW YEAR	7
HINDUISM	16
THE FESTIVAL OF HOLI	17
ISLAM	24
RAMADAN AND THE FESTIVAL OF ID UL-FITR	25
SIKHISM	36
THE FESTIVAL OF DIWALI	37
JUDAISM	44
THE FESTIVAL OF CHANUKAH	45
CHRISTIANITY	52
THE FESTIVAL OF CHRISTMAS	53
A CALENDAR OF FESTIVALS	60

Festivals

A festival is a special time. It is a day or a group of days when thousands of people have a celebration. People dress up in their best clothes. They cook special food. Children are allowed to stay up late.

In hot countries, there is often music and dancing through the streets. In colder countries the celebrations take place inside.

But they are just as happy and exciting.

Festivals are sometimes part of a religious event. They are a chance for people to thank their God for the things He has given them.

And they are a time when people try hard to make up arguments. It is often a chance to have a new start.

Confucianism

Confucianism was begun by **Confucius,** in China three thousand years ago. Confucius is known as a great and wise teacher. He is thought to have written four books. His best known book is **The Analects.**

The Festival of Chinese New Year

New Year is Chinese children's favourite festival. It is a time of tremendous fun. The streets are decorated with banners, lanterns and streamers. The air is filled with music. Everyone forgets all the problems of the old year.

Many things have to be done before New Year arrives. First the whole house has to be scrubbed from top to bottom. Then anything that is broken has to be mended and all quarrels have to be made up.

Chinese people believe that their homes are watched over by a kitchen god. His picture hangs on the wall in the kitchen. He can hear and see everything that happens in the house. About a week before New Year he goes to heaven. He has to tell the god of heaven how the people in the house have been behaving.

The family want the kitchen god to say nice things about them. The mother bakes a little feast for him to make him happy. The father puts honey on the god's lips so that he will say only sweet things about the family. Sometimes families have a very bad year. They are worried about what the kitchen god might say. The father tips wine onto the kitchen god's head to make him sleepy so that he will forget what has happened.

On New Year's Eve, while the kitchen god is in heaven making his report, the family take down his picture. They burn it. On New Year's Day they will put up a new picture of him.

While their parents are busy cleaning and mending, the children decorate the house. They put up red silk and satin streamers. They also make red paper banners and pin them up on the doors. These are supposed to bring good luck.

Red is a very important colour to Chinese people. They believe that it will drive out bad luck and bring in good luck.

The evening of the Chinese New Year is a very exciting time for everyone. Children are allowed to stay up late so they can be at the New Year's dinner.

There is special food to eat, and dumplings that have money inside them.

When they have finished eating, the family goes out to watch the New Year procession. In London the procession goes through Soho, which is where a lot of Chinese people live and work.

Nowadays the procession is for fun but it does have a story behind it.

There is a town in China called Shanghai. Many years ago the people who lived there were being troubled by a terrible monster. The monster only came once every 365 days.

It came in winter when it was very cold and there was very little food to eat. The monster would destroy people's homes. It would eat their crops.

The poor people did not know what to do about the monster. It was so big and powerful they could not fight it.

Then one year they discovered that the monster was frightened of loud noises and of the colour red. So they waited 365 days until it was time for the monster to come again.

Then they hung red cloths on their doors. They made a lot of noise, banging on drums and letting off fireworks.
It worked. The monster was frightened. It did not come near the town.

Nowadays, someone dresses up as the monster to lead the procession. Everyone else makes a lot of noise with music and drums.

You may have seen this procession on television. It is very brightly coloured because of the clothes people wear.
The clothes are always red, yellow or orange. There are also lanterns and decorations hanging in the streets.

There is always a lion which does a special dance. One man is inside the lion costume. Another walks along in front, banging a drum.

There are little red packets hanging from the shops. Inside the packets there is some money. Next to the red packets is a lettuce. The people who own the shops have put them there. The lion has to stretch up and take the money and the lettuce. He pretends to eat the money.

He throws the lettuce back onto the front of the shop.
This is to bring good luck. All the money the lion collects is sent off to a charity.

As well as the lion, every year there is another, different, animal in the procession.
Not a real animal, of course, but someone dressed up in a costume. This is because each Chinese year is named after a different animal.

There is a very old story that tells why.

Once, thousands of years ago, when it was nearly time for New Year, twelve animals were sitting in a group. They were having an argument. There was a dog, a pig, a rat, an ox, a tiger, a rabbit, a dragon, a snake, a horse, a goat, a monkey and a rooster.

'I think the New Year should have a name,' said the dog.

'Yes. It should be called Tiger, after me,' said the tiger.

'No!' shouted the dog and the dragon and the monkey all together. 'It should be named after me.' Soon they were having a terrible argument. They were all shouting and bellowing. They were making such a noise that they disturbed the gods.

The gods suddenly appeared in the sky above them.
The animals were very frightened. 'Why are you making such a terrible noise?' the gods asked. They sounded very angry.

'We were trying to give the New Year a name,' all the animals shouted up at once.

The gods were even angrier. The animals were all shouting and the noise was deafening. 'We can't understand what you are saying when you make such a noise,' they said, still sounding cross. 'You are being very rude.'

The animals felt ashamed of themselves. One at a time, they politely explained what they were arguing about.

'Well,' said the gods, 'there is only one way to settle this. You'd better have a race across the river. Whoever gets there first will have the year named after him.'

The ox was very excited when he heard the news. He knew he was the strongest swimmer. He was bound to win.

When the gods shouted 'Go!' all the animals jumped into the river with a huge splash. They started to swim as hard as they could for the other side.

Of course the ox, because he was biggest and strongest, went into the lead straight away. The rat was next to the ox. He saw that the ox was going to win.

The rat was panting and exhausted, but he swam as hard as he could. Just when he thought he wouldn't be able to swim another stroke, he managed to stretch out and grab a piece of the ox's coat.

The rat pulled hard. He dragged himself onto the ox's tail. He wanted to lie down because he was tired. He made himself crawl a few more steps, up the ox's back and onto his head. Then he lay down, panting. The ox did not know he was there. He carried on swimming strongly for the bank. He was almost there.

Then the ox made a mistake. He looked over his shoulder and saw that he was a long way ahead of the others. He was very excited. He shouted out loud. But, as he shouted, he gulped down a huge mouthful of river water and started to choke. The rat took his chance. He leapt from the ox's head and onto the river bank.

'Hooray! I'm the winner!' he squeaked, jumping up and down.

The poor ox couldn't believe it.

So the gods told the rat that he could have the first year named after him. The second year would be the year of the ox. And, as each animal arrived, they were told their turn to have a year named after them.

Every Chinese person knows the name of the year they were born in. When, every twelve years, their animal comes around again, they are very pleased. It means that they should have a lucky year.

The date of Chinese New Year varies a little each year but is always in January or February.

Hinduism

Hinduism has been a religion for 5,000 years. It began in India. There are several gods. There are gods of nature, gods of battle, gods who created and gods who destroyed. One of the most popular is **Indra,** who is a warrior who fights against evil. The most important god is **Brahma.** Brahma can change himself into other gods. He can change himself into **Siva,** the destroyer and **Vishnu** the preserver and god of love. Vishnu can change himself into other gods, too. For example, **Rama** and **Krishna.**

The River Ganges is holy to Hindus, and hundreds of thousands of people bathe in it every day and sip the river's holy water. Cows are also holy to Hindus because they are living symbols of Mother Earth.

The Festival of Holi

Holi is a Hindu festival. It takes place in spring. It began in northern India and it is still very popular there. Children like Holi because it is great fun.

In the morning they get water pistols and squeezy plastic bottles. They fill them up with coloured water. They put bags of red powder into their pockets and then they go out into the streets. When they see someone coming along, they squirt them with their water pistols. Or they throw some of the red powder on them.

It isn't just the children who do this. Grown ups do it too.

And everyone can be squirted. Even visitors to the country. Hotel staff have to stop tourists and tell them about Holi. They tell them not to go out in their best clothes.

They tell them to go back and change. Otherwise it would be a shock for the visitors to find themselves soaked with red water and with red powder in their hair.

Buses drive along with their windows open. The people on the bus squirt the people outside. The people outside try and squirt them back but it is difficult to aim through the bus window.

By the middle of the morning, everyone has been squirted. There is a lot of noise because everyone is laughing and chasing each other around.

Because Holi is in spring, it is warm. In a few more weeks it would be very hot and no one would feel like running around. The trees are bursting with beautiful coloured flowers. Everything is very bright and happy.

At school the children jump out on their teachers. They have buckets full of coloured water and they throw them at their teachers. Or they bring their water pistols and squirt them. But they have to run away quickly because the teachers try and get them back.

Later on it is time for the processions. There is singing and dancing in the streets.

In the evening a huge Holi bonfire is lit. This is a very important fire. It is sacred. Everyone gives fuel for it. When it is burning well, the ashes from the fire are wiped onto each person's forehead. This is to bring good luck for the year.

Then all the babies who were born after last Holi are brought to the front.

Their mothers carry them around the Holi fire. This is to give the baby strength and to protect it from evil.

Holi is different in England, of course. People can't run around throwing coloured water on other people. If they weren't Hindu they wouldn't understand. They would probably be very upset to be soaked.

European Hindus celebrate in their homes. They make special Holi food, with curries and sweets. But they build the Holi bonfire. They roast coconuts on it to share with everyone.

There are a lot of stories to explain why Holi began.

One of the best known is about a mighty king. He was called Hiranya Kashipu. He once ruled the earth.

He was a terrible, selfish man. He treated his people badly. He got so big-headed in the end that he said he was God. He told all his people that they must worship him.

Everyone was very angry. Even the king's son was angry. His name was Prahlad. He worshipped Brahma. All the people worshipped Brahma. The king was furious with Prahlad.

'How dare you disobey me?' he shouted. 'If you don't obey me I will kill you.'

'You can try,' Prahlad said, quietly. 'But I know Vishnu will protect me.'

Remember that Vishnu was one of the gods Brahma could change himself into. Vishnu was the preserver and the god of love.

The king tried several ways of terrifying Prahlad so that he would do as he was told. Prahlad took no notice.

So, in the end the king decided to kill Prahlad.

The king's sister, Holika, wanted Prahlad to be killed, too. She thought her brother was right. Holika believed she had special powers and could not be burned by fire.

She had an idea. Holika told the king to build a bonfire. She sat in the middle of it. She put Prahlad on her lap.

She expected him to be burned to death. But when the flames died down the king found that Holika had been burned to death and Prahlad was safe.

This is why Hindus build Holi fires. They put images of Holika in the middle of them.

Another story about Holi is about Lord Krishna. Lord Krishna was another of the gods that Brahma could turn himself into. Lord Krishna was very handsome.

All the girls who met him fell in love with him. Each one hoped he would love her because she thought he was the most handsome man in the world.

Lord Krishna loved a girl called Radha. It was the day of the first full moon of spring. Krishna was playing his flute.

The girls were dancing and swirling to the music. They were wearing brightly coloured clothes and looked very beautiful.

Krishna called to Radha. He started to throw red, yellow and green powder at her. Radha laughed and started to throw it back. Soon everyone joined in.

Everyone was covered in the bright colours. There was the music of the flute, and dancing and laughing.

People say that is how the festival of Holi began.
It is a celebration of the happiness Krishna brought.
And a celebration of his love for Radha.

There are a lot more stories about how Holi began.
Holi is celebrated differently in different parts of India.
In some places the festival goes on for as long as eight days.
Sometimes it only lasts for one or two days.

Sometimes the Holi bonfires are at the beginning.
Sometimes they are at the end.

Holi is always a time of joy, a time for forgiving enemies and becoming friends. And a time for everyone to be treated equally.

The date of Holi varies a little from year to year although it is always in February or March.

Islam

The religion of the Muslims is called **Islam**. **Muhammad** began it in the town of Mecca in Arabia 1400 years ago. Although they are not really religious symbols, the **star** and the **crescent moon** are used a great deal in Islamic lands. Muslims worship **Allah** and calligraphy about Allah is holy. The holiest of all words is Allah's name. The **Qur'an** (pronounced, as it is sometimes spelt in the West, Koran) is the Muslim holy book. Muslims believe that this book was written in heaven and revealed to Muhammad by Allah. It has 114 sections and 6,200 verses.

Ramadan and
The Festival of Id ul-Fitr

The description of Ramadan takes the form of a story.

Layla was excited. She couldn't stand still. She was supposed to be helping her mother with the bread for *suhur,* the special meal they would have later, but she was spilling the flour everywhere. 'Layla,' said her mother crossly, 'why won't you stop jumping around?'

'Because I'm so excited,' said Layla. 'Tonight is the beginning of Ramadan and Ramadan is my favourite month of the whole year.'

'Go and find your brothers. Tell them it is time to go to the desert. You're no help in here,' said Layla's mother. But she didn't really sound cross this time.

Layla went outside and called to her brothers who were chasing each other across the sand.

She could only just see them because it was already getting dark.

'It's time to get ready,' she yelled. She could hear the excitement in her voice.

Ahmed came first with Ishmael racing after him.
'Who said?' they demanded.

'I did,' said their father, suddenly appearing in the doorway. 'Get yourselves ready now, or the new moon will be up before we get there.'

The small group walked quickly through the gathering darkness, down the street and out into the desert.

There were hundreds of people already there, sitting in groups as far as Layla could see. She saw some of her friends and called to them excitedly.

The family found a good place to sit and spread the rug they had brought with them. There were people all around them and the buzz of voices was loud.

Layla and her brother peered up into the sky. 'I'm going to fast for the whole of Ramadan this year,' said Ahmed. His voice sounded funny because his head was bent back so far.

Fasting. Layla groaned quietly to herself. That was the hard thing about Ramadan.

Most adults were not allowed to eat or drink anything between sunrise and sunset. The children also had to fast, but not for so long.

It wasn't so bad in winter when the days were shorter and cooler. But when Ramadan was in summer it was very difficult. It was hard to go for hours without a drink, even.

'I'm going to fast all day, every day for the whole month,' said Ishmael.

Layla listened anxiously. If her father let Ishmael fast the whole day, then he would expect her too as well. Ishmael was, after all, two years younger than her.

'No Ishmael, not this year, said her father. 'Wait until you are older. It is not good for young bodies to put such a strain on them.'

'What about you, Layla?' said her mother. 'How long will you fast?'

'Seven hours each day,' said Layla.

'Good,' said her father. 'And then next year perhaps you can manage a little longer.'

Layla didn't want to think about fasting. 'I think I can see the moon,' she said.
'Where, where?' shouted her brothers.

'There.' Layla pointed her finger.
'That's an aeroplane,' said Ahmed scornfully.

But, all across the desert, as the dark settled around them, people became silent and watchful.

Thousands of heads were craned back as thousands of eyes searched the sky.

'I am so glad it isn't cloudy,' Layla whispered. 'I hate not being able to see the moon rise.' That had happened last year and the family had to wait for an announcement on the radio to know that Ramadan had begun.

It was hard to tell who spotted the moon first. A great shout went up across the desert and was echoed in the town where many Muslims were sitting out on rooftops.

People hugged each other and shouted congratulations. Ramadan had begun.

They hurried home so that Layla's father could ring his brother, who lived in London. He was waiting anxiously for the call because skies in England were rainy and cloudy and they could not see the moon.

Then it was time for prayers. Layla's family, like all Muslims, prayed five times a day. Sometimes they went to the mosque with their father, but usually they prayed at home.

That evening, Layla concentrated harder than ever on her prayers.

Ramadan was a very holy time and she wanted to be a good Muslim by praying hard.

The next day began very early because, during Ramadan, the family had to finish eating before the sun rose.

The children were sleepy and it was difficult to eat *suhur* when it felt like the middle of the night still.

'Eat, eat,' their father urged them. 'Remember there will be nothing more for a long time.'

Layla groaned, loudly enough for her father to hear.

'Why do we fast, Layla? he asked her, a little sharply.

'Because it is a sign that we have submitted our bodies and minds to Allah,' Layla said, anxiously. She did not want her father to think that she was not a good Muslim.

Then their father started to talk about the Angel Gabriel's visit to the Prophet Muhammad, but Ishmael interrupted.

'I know what happened, I know what happened,' he shouted.

Their father smiled. 'Tell us,' he said.

'Muhammad was a trader who travelled the land,' Ishmael began eagerly, 'and he met many drunken and badly behaved people who worshipped idols and fought with each other. It made him very upset so he used to go off on his own to a cave to think.'

'And one day,' interrupted Layla, who wanted to show that she knew the story well, too, 'the Angel Gabriel came to him in a vision. Gabriel commanded him to recite the words God had given.'

'And what did those words become?' Her father was looking pleased now, and Layla felt happy again.

'They became the Qur'an, the holy book,' said Layla. 'Then Muhammad, upon whom be peace, tried to tell everyone that there was only one God, Allah, and that worshipping idols was wrong. But no one would believe him.'

'But now Islam is a very important religion,' said Ishmael, 'with millions of followers all around the world.'

'Good.' Their father looked pleased. 'And why are there no pictures of Allah?'

'Because it is written in the Qur'an that an angel will not go into a house where there are pictures. The Prophet Muhammad said that if you must draw pictures then draw pictures of trees and objects that do not have a soul. Instead we write Allah's name as beautifully as we can because it is an honour to write it.'

'The sun will be rising soon,' warned Layla's mother.

'Quick, who's got the threads?' squealed the children, scrabbling around.

Ahmed, because he was the oldest, took the threads, one white and one black, to the window. As soon as there was enough light to see which one was which everyone had to stop eating. The adults would have no more food and no more drink until the sun set and the children would also fast for many hours.

That was the pattern for Ramadan. Each day the family got up in the dark, ate as much as they could of the sugary food Layla's mother provided, and then the adults went through the long hot day without anything to eat or drink. The children fasted, too, but not for as long.

They could not even watch television to take their minds off their hunger pangs.

During Ramadan, people are not allowed to watch television, or go to the cinema or have parties. Instead they read the Qur'an and think about Allah.

As the weeks of the fast passed Layla got more and more excited. The last day of Ramadan, Id ul-Fitr was the most exciting day of the year.

Layla, who had made herself a calendar of the month, crossed off the final day.

'I can't believe it,' she said to her mother. 'Id ul-Fitr is tonight!'

'I know,' said her mother. 'And there is a lot of work to be done. You must spend today helping me with the cooking and cleaning.'

Layla did not mind. It would be something to fill in the hours before Id began.

Layla and her mother went into town to buy food for the next day's feast. All around them were signs of approaching Id: shops crammed full of Id day cards and presents, men climbing ladders to string lines of lights across the street and around buildings.

And people everywhere, rushing to finish their shopping. The whole family had to buy new clothes because no one would wear old things on Id day. And, because there would be huge family parties, there was a lot of food to buy.

Even though the shops had been open all night for the past week there were still huge crowds in town, all bumping into each other.

Layla was very glad when her mother said it was time to go home. They spent the day baking bread, spicing meat and making sweets ready for the next day.

Layla felt sorry for her mother, who was still fasting. It must be very difficult to prepare food for the family each day when you cannot eat until night. And much more difficult today, when the food they were making was so delicious.

After evening prayers Layla and her family set off for town. No one would bother about bedtime tonight!

There were hundreds of people milling around in the streets. Layla saw her friends and called excitedly to them.

Ishmael and Ahmed climbed up onto the balcony of a tall building and leant over the edge, staring into the sky, watching for the new moon. Layla stood on the ground calling up to them.

More and more people began to fill the streets and gradually silence settled on the crowd. It must be almost time for the moon! It was as if all the thousands of people were holding their breath and waiting.

Then a huge shout went up. The new moon had appeared. Ramadan was over!

The lights that had been hung around the buildings and streets suddenly burst on, making the town glitter and gleam like a huge jewel. And everywhere laughing, shouting people hugged each other and shouted congratulations.

Life would return to normal. Layla and her family, along with millions of Muslims all around the world, had faced the challenge of Ramadan and survived.

Ramadan is 11 days earlier each year so, over a period of time, it comes in every season.

Sikhism

Guru Nanak began this religion in India 400 years ago. Sikhs believe in one God. His name is **Eternal Truth.** He is the maker of all things and He lives in all things.

There is a two-edged sword called the **Khanda** which is holy. It has two edges so that it can cut through ignorance and superstition. There are two more swords which are holy. They are called **Kirpans** and they are to defend the truth. A circle called **chakra** is also holy. It reminds people of one God. The sacred book is called the **Guru Granth Sahib.** The book is treated as a living thing. It is opened ceremoniously every morning and put to rest each evening.

The Festival of Diwali

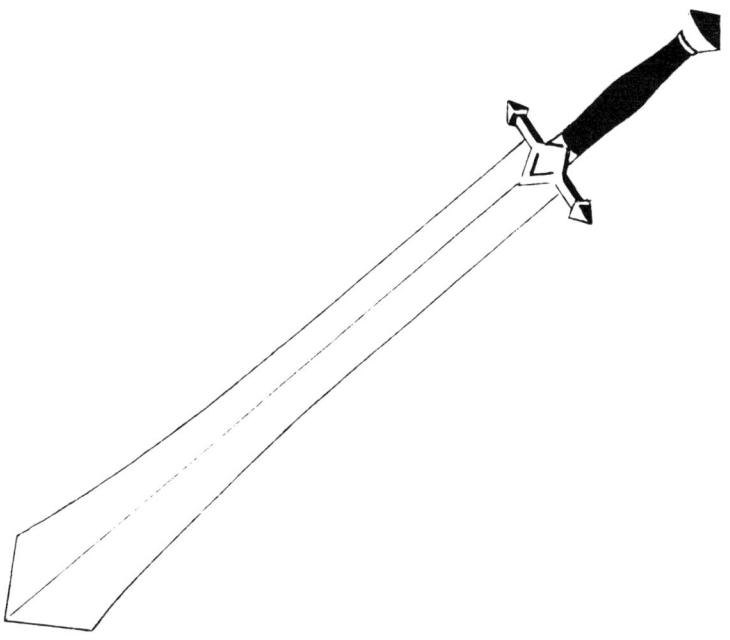

Diwali is a special time for Sikhs. In India thousands of people go to the Golden Temple in Amritsar. The temple is covered in lamps and candles especially for Diwali. It looks very beautiful.

There is a moat around the temple. The lights shine into it and make a bright reflection.

All around the world, Sikhs decorate their homes with strings of fairy lights and lamps and candles.

The lights shine out into the night. They are there to remember a very brave boy. He lived in India nearly four hundred years ago. His name was Guru Hargobind.

A guru is a religious teacher.

At that time India was ruled by the Mughals. They were Muslims. Their leader was called Emperor Jehangir. Jehangir wanted the Sikhs to become Muslims.

Guru Hargobind's father refused. He was tortured and killed by the Mughals.

Emperor Jehangir said to Hargobind, 'We want you to become a Muslim.'

'I will not do that,' said Hargobind. 'My father died rather than stop being a Sikh. I would rather die too.'

The Emperor was angry but he let Hargobind go.
Guru Hargobind was only eleven years old but he decided to fight the Mughals.

He put on two swords, one on either side of him. One was to show that Guru Hargobind was a political leader. The other was to show that he was a religious leader.

Then he went up and down the land, gathering together a great army who would fight the Mughals.

Emperor Jehangir was beginning to feel worried.
Guru Hargobind was becoming very powerful and he was popular with the people.

One night, when Guru Hargobind was sleeping, soldiers arrived. The soldiers arrested Guru Hargobind.

They pushed him into a carriage. Then they drove off into the night until they arrived at a fort in Gwalior.

Guru Hargobind was kept there for a long time. Some people say for two years, some people say for five years. His crime was plotting against the Mughals.

He was kept in a cold, damp room at the bottom of the fort.

There were other people in the prison. There were fifty-two princes in the rooms nearby. It was a very hard, sad time for Guru Hargobind.

He did not have enough to eat and he was always cold. A lot of people in the prison died of hunger and disease.

Guru Hargobind kept praying. He was sure that God would rescue him.

In the end his prayers were answered. One day Emperor Jehangir ordered his release. The Emperor believed that Guru Hargobind's will had been broken and that he would have lost his power over the people.

Guru Hargobind was very glad to be given his freedom but he was worried about the princes.

'I will not leave unless the princes are allowed to leave as well,' he told the guards.

The guards did not know what to do. Prisoners did not usually refuse to leave.

In the end they thought of a plan.

'You can take as many princes as will fit through the corridor of the prison holding onto your clothes,' they said.

Guru Hargobind knew what they were trying to do.

The passages through the prison were very narrow. There would be room for only two people side by side.

Then he had a brilliant idea.

He asked for a dressmaker to be brought to him.
He asked the dressmaker to make a special cloak. It had two very long tassels that reached back for several metres.

Guru Hargobind was pleased with the cloak. It was just what he needed.

All the princes stood in a line. They held onto the tassels and then filed out of the prison.

The guards were very angry but there was nothing they could do. Guru Hargobind had done what they had ordered.

Guru Hargobind went back home and there he saw a wonderful sight.

The Sikhs had filled every house with candles to celebrate his release and to welcome him home.

So that is why there are so many lights shining out into the night during Diwali. And why fireworks light up the sky.

They stand for freedom. The freedom to think what you want to think. The freedom to praise your own God. And the freedom to fight to defend your rights.

In India the festival lasts for five days. In European countries, Diwali usually lasts only one day.

Everyone dresses up in new clothes because Diwali is a time for a new beginning. Diwali is also a time when people make up quarrels.

During the day the streets are filled with music and dancing. Everyone is out enjoying the fun and meeting up with friends.

In the evening all the families have a special Diwali supper. The rooms are filled with candles. After supper there are firework parties that go on late into the night.

The date of Diwali varies a little from year to year but is always in Ocbober or November.

Judaism

Abraham founded this religion in Palestine four thousand years ago. Jews believe in one God, called **JHVH** (Yahweh) and they worship Him in a **synagogue.**

The symbols of Judaism are the **Shield (Star) of David** and the **Menorah** (which is an eight-branched lamp). Its sacred writings are the **Torah** ('Law'), the **Prophets** and **Psalms,** the **Talmud** and the **Gemara.**

The Festival of Chanukah

Chanukah is a Jewish festival of light. Chanukah celebrates a great battle more than two thousand years ago.

This was when Antiochus Epiphanes was the Emperor of Syria. He was a very cruel man. He wanted the Jews in Syria to follow the same religion as he did. He tried to force Jews to obey his laws.

The Jews tried hard to disobey him, but the Emperor was a powerful man. He became very angry with the Jews. He made a new law.

Jews were forbidden to read their books. They could not observe their holy days, or pray to their God. The Emperor sent his soldiers to the Temple, the holiest Jewish place. They caused terrible damage.

The Jews were very upset and angry but there was nothing they could do. The Emperor was too powerful.

Syrian soldiers went throughout the land, telling Jews of the Emperor's new laws.

Eventually, the news reached a village called Modin. A priest called Mattathias lived there. He had five sons.

Mattathias was angry when he heard about the new laws. He and his sons decided that they would fight for the freedom of their people.

One of the sons was called Judah. He formed a small army of local men. They were called the Maccabees. Judah led the Maccabees into many desperate battles. They fought the Syrians up in the mountains and on farmland. They fought right across the country.

Judah and the Maccabees were untrained and had to find their own weapons, but they began to win the battles against the Syrian soldiers. More and more people came to join Judah in his great struggle.

They fought for three years. In the end the Maccabees pushed the Syrian army right out of their land. The Jews were free again. The people hurried to Jerusalem to clean the Temple. The Syrian soldiers had done terrible things. They had put up a pagan altar and filled the Temple with unclean animals.

And the menorah, a huge lamp with seven branches, had been put out. The lamp was supposed always to be alight, and shine out for people during the hours of darkness. The Syrian soldiers had extinguished its flame.

The Jews searched and searched for the special, pure oil that had to be used in the lamp. But all they could find was a tiny amount.

It was just enough to keep the menorah burning for one night. They were very upset. It would take them eight days to make some new oil. But they lit the menorah and gathered around it to say prayers.

Then a miracle happened. The menorah, with just the tiny amount of oil, kept burning for eight days and nights, until the people could make new oil.

That is why Chanukah lasts for eight days, one for each of the days the lamp burned. Jewish people have their own menorahs for Chanuka. Some people have old lamps and some people have modern ones. Sometimes the lamps burn oil, sometimes they have candles. Most lamps have eight branches and on each night of Chanukah another branch of the lamp is lit until, by the eighth day, all eight are burning.

Chanukah is in November or December, when it gets dark early. So people passing Jewish homes can see the lamp's light shining out into the night for a long time.

Although there are many important festivals for Jews, Chanukah is probably the children's favourite. Eight days of celebrating means a lot of fun!

Each evening, after the next branch of the menorah is lit, the family sing songs which tell the story of the Maccabees.

Then, while their parents prepare supper, the children play special games.

They gamble, using a top which is called a dreidl or sevivon.

On each side of the top is a Hebrew letter – *Nun, Gimmel, Heh* or *Shin.*

These letters stand for the words *Nes Gadol Hayah Sham* which means, 'A great miracle happened there.' (This refers to the miracle at the Temple in Jerusalem when the oil lasted for eight days.)

Each child has a pile of raisins and almonds, or small amounts of money. Each player has to put some food or money in the centre, and then the children take turns to spin the top.

If the top lands on *Gimmel,* the player wins everything in the centre. If it lands on *Heh,* the player takes half, if it is *Nun,* the player takes nothing. And if it is *Shin* the player has to put more of her or his pile into the middle. Eventually someone wins everything, by which time supper is ready.

At Chanukah people eat delicious potato pancakes, called latkes and also doughnuts called savganiot.

Best of all, from the children's point of view, are the presents. Because each day of Chanukah is important, children can get presents on any of the eight nights.

Some parents give their children something on every night. Some parents give one or two presents for the whole holiday.

In Israel, the Festival of Light, as the time of Chanukah is known, is a very important time. In the town of Modin, where Judah and the Maccabees lived, there is a special celebration.

The people who live there light a torch. Then runners carry it for eighty kilometres, all the way to the Knesset, the Israeli Parliament, which is in Jerusalem. The torch spreads light on its journey. It reminds everyone who sees it of the time Judah saved the Jewish people from a terrible darkness.

The date of Chanukah varies slightly from year to year but is always in November or December.

Christianity

Christianity began nearly 2000 years ago in Palestine. The religion was founded by **Jesus Christ.**

There are several symbols of Christianity. The oldest is the **fish** but the best known is the **cross.** The Christian sacred book is the **Bible.** Christians believe in one God, who sent His son Jesus Christ to earth.

The Festival of Christmas

There are many millions of Christians around the world. To each of them Christmas is a very special time.

It is the Christian festival of light. It lasts for twelve days. Christmas Day is on 25 December. This is the day when Christians celebrate the birth of Jesus Christ.

The birth of Jesus is important to Christians because it was a sign of God coming to earth. Christians believe that Jesus was a person and God.

The Bible says that when Jesus was born he brought the light of God with him.

Jesus was born in Bethlehem. No one knows the actual day Jesus was born.

Christians chose 25 December because it was already a special day. It was the day when people worshipped the sun. It was the shortest day, and so it was the day with the least light.

Christians used this day to thank the sun for the summer that had passed. And they prayed that the sun would come back and give them another summer.

The calendar has changed since that time. Now the shortest day is on 21 December, but Christmas Day stayed on 25 December.

Christmas is a very big, happy celebration. There are four weeks to get ready for it. This time is called Advent. Advent means 'The Coming'. It is an exciting time for Christians.

Christians burn Advent candles and children hang Advent calendars in their homes. Each day they open one of the doors on the calendar. The biggest door is for Christmas Eve.

In Britain, Christians go carol singing. Carol singing usually starts in the middle of December. People go from house to house singing carols and collecting money for charity.

They carry torches and lanterns so that they can find their way in the dark. They knock on doors and people hurry to open them and hear the carols.

They put some money in the collection tin. Sometimes they give the carol singers sweet pastries called mincepies.

At Christmas people decorate their houses. They put up a Christmas tree. It is a fir tree which is decorated with bright sparkling balls and chains of lights. Underneath the Christmas tree people pile presents for their family and friends. Everyone opens their presents on Christmas Day.

On the walls and mantlepieces there are Christmas cards from friends and relatives and the rooms are decorated with paper streamers.

Children hang stockings up in their bedrooms on Christmas Eve. They hope that Father Christmas will come down the chimney in the middle of the night and fill the stockings with presents.

Many Christians go to church on Christmas morning. The church is decorated with holly, flowers and candles. It looks beautiful.

After the church service everyone goes home to open presents and eat a huge feast. Christmas Day is a very happy day, with big, noisy family parties.

Christians in other countries celebrate Christmas in different ways. Here are some examples.

In Italy, the main celebration is Midnight Mass. This is a church service on the night before Christmas Day. The churches are crowded with people. Sometimes there is not enough room for everyone. Some people have to stand outside and listen to loudspeakers. But everyone tries to get inside at the end of the service.

They want to visit the crib which has a model of the baby Jesus in it. They say a prayer over the crib.

Christmas Day is very quiet. Italians do not give each other presents. But on Epiphany, which is on 6 January, everything changes. This is the day when Italians celebrate the coming of the Wise Men. They were the three kings who followed a star to the place where Jesus was born.

It is the day when Italian Catholics have family parties. It is also the day when Befana the witch comes. She calls at each house. She brings a horrible sweet for children who have been naughty and presents for children who have been good.

In Finland it is dark practically all day in December. On Christmas Eve people visit the graves of relatives. They put candles on the graves. Then, at night, everyone goes to church. Afterwards they go home for a family party. They open presents and eat and drink. They stay up until very late at night.

In the Lebanon, Christmas is a very religious time. The church service lasts for five hours on Christmas Eve. The church is full of candles. There are candles around a crib which has a model of the baby Jesus in it.

Late at night everyone goes home to a big family party. The party goes on for most of the night. In the morning everyone goes back to church.

The church looks wonderful and the priest is wearing special red and gold clothes. He has a huge, jewelled cross around his neck.

Even though it is the special Christmas Day service, it is very quiet. Everyone is tired because they have had hardly any sleep.

Families bring a loaf of bread with them. The bread is called Erbani. The priest blesses it and the families eat the bread at lunchtime.

In the islands of the Caribbean not all the people are Christians, but everyone joins in the Christmas celebrations. They start to get ready for Christmas in November.

Families begin to bake puddings, bread and cakes. They make sorrell juice, which is a delicious spicy blackcurrant drink. They also make ginger beer.

This is a very happy time and everyone helps with the work.

On Christmas Day families gather for a huge meal. The main part of it is spiced chicken or pork. The family parties get very noisy.

Then everyone goes out on the streets. It is hot and sunny. They carry on the party outside, and watch the parade.

It is full of colour and noise. People wear bright costumes.

They dance and sing. There are African drums and calypso steel bands. Lots of children are in the parade. They wear fancy dress and dance along the streets.

The ways of celebrating Christmas around the world are quite different. But all the celebrations have a serious message. They remember the day Jesus Christ came into the world.

Christmas Day is on 25 December.

A calendar of Festivals

This calendar is intended as a quick reference guide. Because of the differences between the lunar and solar calendar, each year some festivals are on different dates. Movable festivals have been marked in italics.
The asterisks mark festivals described in this book.

January
1   New Year (Gregorian calendar)
6   Epiphany (Christian)
19 Epiphany (Russian Orthodox)

January/February
*Chinese New Year (Yuan Tan)**
New Year for Trees (Tu Bishvat) (Jewish)
Maghi (Sikh)

February
Parinirvana (Mahayana) (Buddhist)
Sarasvati Puja (Hindu)
Shiva Ratri (Hindu)
Pongal (Hindu)

February/March
Shrove Tuesday Mardi Gras (Christian)
Purim (Lots) (Jewish)
Lantern Festival End of New Year (Chinese)
Holi (Hindu)*
Hola-Mohalla (Sikh)

March
3 Hina Matsiri (Japan)
17 St Patrick's Day (Ireland)
  Ramanavmi (Hindu)

March/April
  Easter (Christian)
  Passover (Jewish)

April
4 Ch'ing Ming (Chinese)
13 Baisakhi (Sikh)

April/May
  Hindu New Year

May
1 May Day Festivals and International Labour Day
  Dragon Boat Festival (Chinese)

May/June
  Thirty-third day of Omer (Jewish)
  Jerusalem Day (Jewish)
  The Feast of Weeks (Jewish)

June/July
  Ratha Jatra (Hindu)

July
13 Obon (Japanese Shinto/Buddhist)

July/August
Festival of Maidens (Chinese)

August
Raksha Bandham (Hindu)
Anniversary of Guru Granth Sahib (Sikh)
Yue Lan (Chinese Tao)
Chung Yuan (Chinese Buddhist)

August/September
Janmashtami (Hindu)
Ganesh Chaturthi (Hindu)
Rakhsha Bandham (Hindu)

September/October
Chung Ch'iu (Chinese)
Ch'ung Yeung (Chinese)
Durga Puja (Hindu)
Harvest Festivals (Christian)
Navaratra (Hindu)
Rosh Hashanah (Jewish)
Simchat Torah (Jewish)
Succot (Jewish)
Yom Kippur (Jewish)

October
Dashara (Hindu)

October/November
Diwali (Hindu/Sikh)*

November
15 Shichi-go-san (Japan)
    Thanksgiving Day (USA)

November/December
    Chanukah (Jewish)*

December
8   Bodhi Day (Mahayana Buddhist)
13 St Lucia's Day
24 Christmas Eve (Christian)
25 Christmas Day (Christian)*
31 New Year's Eve. Hogmonay
31 Joya no kane (Japanese Hindu/Shinto)

Ramadan and the Festival of Id ul-Fitr (Muslim)
Ramadan is 11 days earlier each year so, over a period of time, it comes in every season.